Presented to:

_____

From:

_____

Date:

_____

ZONDERKIDZ

The Beginner's Bible® for Toddlers
Copyright © 2007 Zondervan. All Rights Reserved. All *The Beginner's Bible®* copyrights and trademarks
(including art, text, characters, etc.) are owned by Zondervan of Grand Rapids, Michigan.

Requests for information should be addressed to:
Grand Rapids, 5300 Patterson SE, Michigan 49530

Library of Congress Cataloging-in-Publication Data

The beginners Bible for toddlers / Illustrated by Kelly Pulley.
        p. cm. -- (The beginner's Bible)
      "Copyright, Mission City Press"--T.p. verso.
      Included index.
      ISBN-13: 978-0-310-71408-8 (hardcover)
      ISBN-10: 0-310-71408-7 (hardcover)
      1. Bible stories, English. I. Pulley, Kelly. II. Mission City Press.
  BS551.3.D48 2007
  220. '505--dc22
                                                   2006027618

Editor: Kristen Tuinstra
Art direction: Laura Maitner-Mason

Printed in China

---

15 16 17 18 /LPC/ 19 18 17 16

The Beginner's Bible for Toddlers

Illustrated by Kelly Pulley

ZONDERkidz

ZONDERVAN.com/
AUTHORTRACKER
follow your favorite authors

OLD TESTAMENT

NEW TESTAMENT

The Old Testament

Timeless Bible Stories

The Beginning

Genesis 1

In the beginning, the world was empty.
Darkness was everywhere.
But God had a plan!

God created dark nights for sleeping.
He made bright days for playing.

Then God made the big, blue sky and
puffy clouds. Below the sky he added the
big, blue ocean.

Next, God pushed back the waters
and made some dry ground. He made
flowers and trees to grow in the ground.

God put a shining sun in the daytime.
He put a glowing moon and twinkling
stars in the sky for the nighttime.

God made swishy fish and squiggly creatures to live in the ocean. He made birds to fly across the sky. He created animals to creep, crawl, hop, and gallop.

Then God made the best creature—
a person. God named him Adam. God
looked at everything he created and said,
"This is very good!" Then God rested.

The First People

Genesis 2

God planted a garden for Adam.
He loved Adam very much.

Adam loved his new home.
His job was to take care of the garden.

Adam loved all the animals. But he wanted a special friend who was just right for him. So God made a woman.

Adam called her Eve. She was just
right for Adam. They loved each
other. Together they took care of
God's garden.

Noah's Ark

Genesis 6–9

As the world got older, many people were born. They did bad things, and they forgot about God.

Except Noah. Noah loved God.

God was sad that everyone but Noah forgot about him. He told Noah about his plan to start over. "Build an ark," God said. So Noah began building the ark.

When it was done, God said, "Take two of every animal into the ark."

After Noah and the animals were inside,
the rain began to fall. And fall. And fall.
Water covered the whole earth.

Finally, the rain stopped. Everyone
inside the ark was safe and happy.

Noah sent a dove to find land. It flew
and flew but never found any. So it
came back. Soon, Noah sent the dove
out again. This time, it brought back
a leaf. Noah cheered, "It must have
found land!"

When the water dried up, God told Noah
to leave the ark. Noah praised God.

God put a beautiful rainbow in the sky.
It was a sign of his promise to never
flood the whole earth with water again.

A New Home

Genesis 12–17

Just like Noah, Abraham also loved God.
So did his wife Sarah.

One day, God said to Abraham,
"It's time to go to a new place!"
"Let's go," said Abraham.

So along with their helpers, Abraham and Sarah packed up and went. God promised to lead them to a new land that would be theirs forever.

All the land they saw was wonderful.

God said to Abraham, "Count all the stars. You will have as many people in your family as there are stars in the sky. Your family will bless the world!"

Joseph's Coat

Genesis 37–47

Abraham had a grandson named Jacob.
Jacob had a son named Joseph.
Jacob loved Joseph the best of all his sons.

Jacob gave Joseph a colorful coat.
His brothers were mad. They
wanted colorful coats, too!

His brothers didn't like Joseph.
They sent him away to be a slave
in Egypt.

Joseph was very sad.
He didn't want to be a slave.
He even had to go to jail!

When Joseph got older, God sent
someone to help Joseph get out of jail.
Soon, Joseph became a great leader.

One day, Joseph's family went to
Joseph in Egypt for food. They were
very hungry. Joseph forgave his brothers,
and the whole family moved to Egypt.

Baby in a Basket

Exodus 1—2:10

Many years went by. A mean king
named "Pharaoh" ruled over Egypt. He
did not know Joseph, and he did not like
God's people, who were called Israelites.
They loved God.

Pharaoh did not like God.
He made the Israelites work extra hard.
One day, he decided to get rid of all the
Israelite boys.

An Israelite mother wanted to save her
baby boy. So she gently laid him inside
a basket and placed him in the river.

Pharaoh's daughter saw the basket and
peeked inside. "I want to keep you as
my own baby," the princess whispered.
She named him Moses.

The baby's big sister had been
watching nearby. She said to the
princess, "I know a woman who
can help you take care of the baby."
The big sister ran to get her mom.
She took care of Moses.

When Moses was a young boy, he
returned to live with the princess.
He grew up in the palace.

Ten Rules

Exodus 19–20

God led the Israelites to a mountain.
Thunder roared and lightning flashed.

Moses became the leader of the Israelites. One day, God told Moses to go to the top of a mountain. God wanted to give Moses ten rules. God wrote them on tablets of stone.

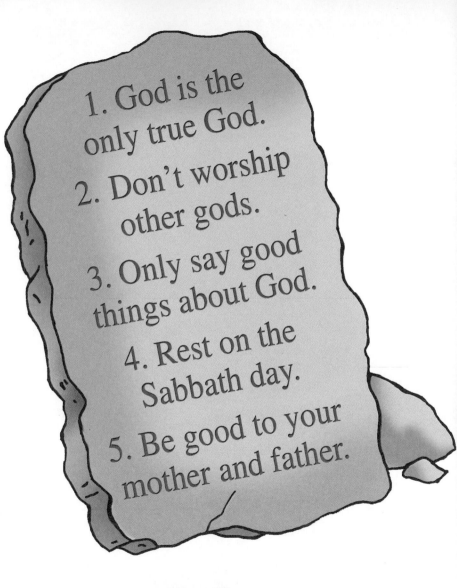

1. God is the only true God.

2. Don't worship other gods.

3. Only say good things about God.

4. Rest on the Sabbath day.

5. Be good to your mother and father.

6. Do not murder.

7. Husbands and wives should always be faithful to each other.

8. Do not steal.

9. Do not tell lies.

10. Never want what belongs to others.

God told Moses to share these rules with
the other Israelites.

The Israelites needed a place to
worship God. They built a special
tent called a tabernacle.

The Mean Giant

1 Samuel 17:1–51

Enemies of God wanted to fight the
Israelites. A giant soldier named Goliath
yelled, "Bring out your best soldier to
fight me!"

The Israelites were afraid. They did not want to fight the giant.

"I am not afraid to fight the giant,"
said a young boy named David.
The king said, "You can't fight the
giant. You are too small."
David said, "God will be with me."

David picked up some stones.
"One, two, three, four, five," he said.
The giant laughed at David.
David said, "I am not scared. God will
help me fight you."

David put a stone in his sling and
ran toward the giant. Then he let
the stone fly.

The stone hit Goliath's
forehead, and he fell to the
ground. The Israelites won!

The Brave Queen

Esther 1–10

Esther was an Israelite and very beautiful.
Since she was so beautiful, a king chose
Esther to be his queen.

Esther was raised by her cousin. Esther and her cousin loved God very much.

Haman was the king's helper.
He wanted everyone to bow down to
him. But Esther's cousin would only
bow down to God. Haman decided to
destroy the Israelites.

Esther was scared, but she had to do
something. She was in danger, and so
were all the Israelites. She prayed to
God to help her come up with a plan.

At dinner, Esther asked the
king, "Why does Haman want
to get rid of the Israelites? I am
an Israelite. Haman is trying to
get rid of me!"

The king told his guards, "Take Haman
away!" He told Queen Esther,
"I will keep you and the Israelites safe."
God used Esther to save his people!

Daniel and the Lions

Daniel 6

Darius became king of his land.
Daniel helped the king. The king's
other helpers did not like Daniel.

The helpers told the king, "You are such
a great king. You should make a new law
that everyone must pray only to you. If
they don't pray to you, they should be
thrown into the lions' den."

King Darius made the new law,
but Daniel kept praying to God.
Daniel loved God. The king's
helpers caught Daniel praying!

They told King Darius, "Now you
must throw Daniel into the lions' den."
The king knew he had been tricked!
The law was a mistake.

Daniel was thrown into the lions' den.
But he knew God would take care of him.

King Darius said, "I hope your God
will save you." That night, the king
was worried about Daniel.

The next morning, King Darius said,
"Daniel?" Daniel said, "My God sent
his angel to protect me." King Darius
ordered everyone to honor and respect
the God of Daniel.

Jonah and the Big Fish

Jonah 1—3:10

Jonah was a prophet of God. One day, God said, "Go to the city of Nineveh. Tell them to stop doing bad things."

Jonah did not want to go. Instead, he jumped into a boat to sail across the sea. God sent a big storm. They were scared! Jonah told the sailors, "If you throw me into the water, the sea will become calm again."

So the sailors threw Jonah into the
sea. Instantly, the sea became calm.

Just then, Jonah saw a big fish coming.
Gulp! The fish swallowed Jonah.

For three days and nights, Jonah sat
inside the fish. He prayed to God,
"Please forgive me."

Then God told the fish to spit Jonah onto dry land. God told Jonah a second time, "Go and tell the people of Nineveh to stop doing bad things."

This time, Jonah obeyed God.
The people in Nineveh were
sorry for doing bad things, so
God forgave them.

The New Testament

Timeless Bible Stories

An Angel Visits Mary

Luke 1:26–38

God sent the angel Gabriel to visit a young
woman. Her name was Mary. She was
scared. She had never seen an angel before.

Gabriel said, "Don't be afraid.
You are going to have a baby.
You must name him Jesus.
He will be the Son of God."

Mary asked, "How can it be?
I am not married."

Gabriel answered, "With God,
all things are possible."

Mary said, "I love God. I will do
what he has chosen me to do."

Baby Jesus Is Born

Luke 2:1–7

Mary loved Joseph. Joseph and Mary
were going to be married soon.

The leader of the country told everyone
to go back to the town where their
families came from. So Joseph and Mary
went to Bethlehem.

Mary was going to have her baby
very soon. As soon as they arrived in
Bethlehem, they looked for a place to
sleep. But all the inns were full.

Finally, a man helped them. He said, "I do not have any rooms left, but you can sleep in the stable with the animals."

Joseph made a warm place for Mary
to rest. While they were there, baby
Jesus was born.

Mary wrapped up Jesus and
gently laid him in a manger.

Shepherds Visit

Luke 2:8–20

On the night Jesus was born, shepherds
were watching their sheep.
Suddenly, an angel stood before them.

The angel said, "Do not be afraid.
I bring joyful news to all people.
Today, a Savior has been born!
He is sleeping in a manger."

Then a choir of angels appeared.
They sang, "Glory to God in the highest!
Peace and goodwill to everyone on earth!"

The shepherds rushed to find baby Jesus.
They told Joseph and Mary what the
angel said.

As they returned to their sheep, the shepherds told everyone about Jesus. They shouted praises to God!

The Three Visitors

Matthew 2:1–12

When Jesus was born, God put a very bright, special star in the sky. Some wise men who lived far away saw this star.

They knew it was a sign from God that a new king had been born. They followed the star to Bethlehem to visit Jesus.

The wise men found young Jesus. They
worshiped him and gave him gifts fit for
a king: gold, perfume, and sweet spices.

John the Baptist

Matthew 3:1–17; Mark 1:1–11; Luke 3:1–22; John 1:6–34

John was Jesus' cousin. When John grew up, he ate bugs and honey.
John told many people about God. John told them to be kind and tell the truth.

John taught the people that they had done bad things. The people needed to say, "I'm sorry. I'll try not to do those bad things again."

When the people said they were sorry,
John baptized them in a river. The
people were happy to be forgiven.

When Jesus grew up, he came to the river.
John knew Jesus would save them from
their sins. Even though Jesus had never
done bad things, he said, "John, I need to
be baptized by you."

John baptized Jesus in the river. The
Holy Spirit came down from heaven.
It looked like a dove. God said, "This
is my Son, and I love him."

Jesus and His Friends

Matthew 4:18–22; 9:9; 10:1–4;
Mark 1:16–20; 2:14; 3:13–18; Luke 5–6

Jesus began to tell people about God.
He had a lot of work to do, so he
needed to find some helpers.

Jesus walked to the seashore. He found some fishermen. He called to them, "Come. Follow me. I will make you fishers of people."

Right away, they left their
boats to follow Jesus.

Later, Jesus met some more helpers.
They all quit their jobs to follow Jesus.

Soon he had twelve new friends
who helped Jesus teach people
about God's love.

Jesus Teaches People

Matthew 5:1–12; 6:25–34; Luke 6:17–23; 12:22–31

Many people went to see Jesus. Children,
moms, dads, grandmas, and grandpas all
wanted to hear what Jesus was teaching.

"Look at the birds," Jesus said.
"Do they store food for later?
No. God feeds them."

"Look at the flowers," said Jesus. "They don't work or make clothes. God dresses them in leaves and petals."

Then Jesus said, "You are much more important than birds and flowers. Do not worry. God takes care of them, so he will take care of you."

Jesus Calms the Storm

Matthew 8:23–27

Jesus and his friends got into a boat.

Jesus was so tired! He took a nap.

Suddenly a big storm came up.
Waves splashed over the boat.
Wind whipped around the men.

The men woke Jesus up and shouted,
"The boat is sinking! Don't you care?"

Jesus asked, "Why are you so afraid? Don't you have any faith at all?" Then Jesus told the storm to stop. Right away it was calm.

The men were amazed. They said to each other, "Who is this man Jesus? Even the wind and the waves obey him!"

Mary and Martha

Luke 10:38–42

One day Jesus visited his friends
Mary and Martha. Mary sat at his feet
and listened to him for a long time.

Martha was busy.
There was so much to do!

Soon Martha got mad. "I am busy doing everything while Mary is doing nothing! Jesus, please tell my sister to help!"

"Martha," Jesus said, "You should not be upset. Mary is doing what is better. She is listening to me."

The Lost Sheep

Matthew 18:10–14; Luke 15:3–7

Some people wondered who was most important to God. So Jesus told them a story.

"What does a shepherd do? He watches over his sheep. He gives them food and water."

"He counts them to make sure they are all there. If one is lost, he looks for it everywhere."

"The shepherd does not give up. At last, he finds the little lost sheep!"

"He carries the sheep back. He cheers, 'My lost sheep has been found!' "

Then Jesus said, "God is like a shepherd. When someone turns from God, he is very sad. But when the person comes back to God, he is very happy."

Ten Lepers

Luke 17:11–19

As Jesus was traveling, he met ten lepers. Their bodies were covered with sores. The lepers shouted, "Jesus, please heal us!"

Jesus said, "Go. Show yourselves to
the priests." The ten men left. As they
walked away, something amazing
happened. All the men were healed!

But only one man went
back to thank Jesus.

The man said, "Thank you!"
Jesus wondered where the other
men were. The others did not
come back to thank him.

Jesus and the Children

Matthew 19:13–15; Mark 10:13–16; Luke 18:15–17

Moms and dads brought their children
to Jesus so he would bless them.

But the helpers didn't understand.
They said, "Stop. Do not bother Jesus.
He is just too busy."

Jesus told the helpers,
"Don't stop the children.
Let the children come to me."

"You must become like little children
if you want to be with God in heaven."
Then Jesus blessed the children.

A Short Man

Luke 19:1–10

Zacchaeus was a short man. He
collected money from the people
and gave it to the king. He also
took a bit extra for himself.

The people didn't like Zacchaeus
because he took their money.

A crowd of people wanted to see Jesus.
Zacchaeus wanted to see, too, but he
was too short. So he climbed a tree.

As Jesus passed by, he looked up and
said, "Zacchaeus, come down. I want
to go to your house."

Jesus was kind to Zacchaeus. Jesus
changed Zacchaeus' life! He gave
poor people many of his belongings
and paid people back more than what
he had stolen.

The True King

**Matthew 21:1–11; Mark 11:1–11;
Luke 19:29–40; John 12:12–19**

Jesus and his helpers wanted to go to
Jerusalem for a celebration. Jesus told
two helpers to bring him a donkey.

Jesus rode the donkey to Jerusalem.

A big crowd welcomed him.

People waved palm branches and put
them on the road in front of Jesus.

They shouted, "Hosanna! Hosanna!
Blessed is the king of Israel!"

A Poor Woman's Gift

Mark 12:41–44; Luke 21:1–4

Jesus and his helpers watched
people give money to the church.
The people dropped their money
into an offering box.

The rich people put a lot
of money into the box.

Jesus saw a poor woman. She put two
small coins into the box. That was all
she had. "This woman's gift is greater
than all the others," Jesus said to his
helpers.

"She gave *all* the money she had. The rich people gave a lot of money, but they still have lots of money left."

Jesus Is Alive!

Matthew 26–28;
Luke 24:39–40, 50–53; John 13:1

Jesus knew that he had to die
for the sins of all people. It was
part of God's plan.

Soon, it was time.
Jesus died on the cross for our sins.

The people who loved Jesus
were very sad. But they forgot
something that Jesus had said.
He would see them again soon!

Mary Magdalene was walking
with some friends to the grave.

An angel told them, "Do not be
afraid. Jesus is not here. He is alive!"

Later, the women saw Jesus. They worshiped him. He said, "Go tell my helpers I will see them soon." They ran to tell them.

Jesus Returns

John 20:19–20

Soon, Jesus stood in front of his
helpers. "I am not a ghost," Jesus
said. "Touch my hands so you know
it is really me."

He really was alive!
They cheered.
They were very, very
happy to see Jesus again.

Jesus Goes to Heaven

Matthew 28:16–20; Luke 24:44–51; Acts 1:6–11

Jesus brought his helpers to a mountain. "It's time for me to go to heaven now. Tell others about me."

Then Jesus went up to heaven in a
cloud. His helpers stared at the sky
for a long time.

Suddenly, two angels appeared.
"Why are you still standing here?"
they asked. "Jesus will return the
same way you saw him go."

The helpers remembered that Jesus
said he would come back to take them
to heaven. They were very happy.